PERSPECTIVES

An illustrated anthology

HARINIE JEEVITHA

Illustrated by Meghna Unnikrishnan

INDIA • SINGAPORE • MALAYSIA

Notion Press Media Pvt Ltd

No. 50, Chettiyar Agaram Main Road,
Vanagaram, Chennai, Tamil Nadu – 600 095

First Published by Notion Press 2021

ISBN 978-1-68538-348-0

To co-beholders of perspectives
and its parallel universes...

CONTENTS

TRANSLITERATION & PRONUNCIATION GUIDE

(Devanagari, Telugu, Bengali)

Devanagari	Telugu	Bengali	Transliteration	Sounds
अ	అ	অ	a	hut
आ	ఆ	আ	ā	palm
इ	ఇ	ই	i	sit
ई	ఈ	ঈ	ī	seat
उ	ఉ	উ	u	put
ऊ	ఊ	ঊ	ū	rule
ऋ	ఋ	ঋ	ṛ	rhyme
ॠ	ౠ	ৠ	ṝ	rhetoric
ऌ	ఌ	ঌ	ḷ	girl
-	ఎ	-	e	enter
ए	ఏ	এ	ē	ballet
ऐ	ఐ	ঐ	ai	bright
-	ఒ	-	o	code
ओ	ఓ	ও	ō	board
औ	ఔ	ঔ	au	sound
अं	అం	অং	ṃ	drum
अः	అః	অঃ	ḥ	ha*
क	క	ক	ka	kid
ख	ఖ	খ	kha	cricket
ग	గ	গ	ga	good

Devanagari	Telugu	Bengali	Transliteration	Sounds
घ	ఘ	ঘ	gha	egg
ङ	ఙ	ঙ	ṅa	ankle
च	చ	চ	ca	child
छ	ఛ	ছ	cha	watch
ज	జ	জ	ja	jug
झ	ఝ	ঝ	jha	fridge
ञ	ఞ	ঞ	ña	banyan
ट	ట	ট	ṭa	tall
ठ	ఠ	ঠ	ṭha	butter
ड	డ	ড	ḍa	doll
ढ	ఢ	ঢ	ḍha	adhesive
ण	ణ	ণ	ṇa	under
त	త	ত	ta	thesaurus
थ	థ	থ	tha	thick
द	ద	দ	da	this
ध	ధ	ধ	dha	the
न	న	ন	na	neat
प	ప	প	pa	pen
फ	ఫ	ফ	pha	pup
ब	బ	ব	ba	boy
भ	భ	ভ	bha	abhorrent
म	మ	ম	ma	mind
य	య	য	ya/ẏa	yawn

Devanagari	Telugu	Bengali	Transliteration	Sounds
र	ర	র	ra	river
ल	ల	ল	la	luck
व	వ	-	va	victory
श	శ	শ	śa	ship
ष	ష	ষ	ṣa	sugar
स	స	স	sa	smile
ह	హ	হ	ha	hat

*This pronunciation is not fixed. It depends on the syllable following it as well as preceding it.

Note :

a) Sounds are only approximated to English equivalents.

b) The sounds indicated are not exact to Bengali phonology.

c) Kashmiri transliteration has been approximated to its pronunciation.

d) Names of poets are not in transliteration.

TRANSLITERATION & PRONUNCIATION GUIDE

(Tamil)

Tamil	Transliteration	Sounds
அ	a	cut
ஆ	ā	car
இ	i	fit
ஈ	ī	feet
உ	u	bull
ஊ	ū	boon
எ	e	set
ஏ	ē	valet
ஐ	ai	buy
ஒ	o	go
ஓ	ō	goat
ஔ	au	now
ஃ	ah	Bahrain
க	ka/ga	kettle/give
ங	ṅa	ring
ச	cha/sa	chair/sir
ஞ	ña	banyan
ட	ta/da	toy/doll
ண	ṉa	under
த	tha/dha	thick/them

Tamil	Transliteration	Sounds
ந	na	sun
ப	pa/ba	pair/ball
ம	ma	me
ய	ya	yack
ர	ra	road
ல	la	live
வ	va	victory
ழ	zha	Jacques*
ள	ḻa	girl
ற	ṟa	rabbit
ன	ṇa	bunny
ஜ	ja	jug
ஹ	ha	hum

*This sound is approximated to the French pronunciation.

Note :

a) Sounds are only approximated to English equivalents.

b) Names of poets are not in transliteration.

FOREWORD

This volume of poetry heralds the arrival of Kum. Harinie Jeevitha, the Dancer–Poet. All along we have watched her dance to others' words and rhythms; now we hear the rhythms and words that set the tune and pace from within.

When Harinie spoke to me first about her poetry, she confessed that while she works consciously on her dance, practising her technique to perfection, poetry just happens. It is almost as though, she said, the poetry writes itself through her. Well, that is her experiential truth. To us spell-bound watchers of her performance and, now, inquisitive readers of her poetry, a different experience awaits! Her dancing has always seemed effortless as second nature to all her audience. A lot of practice, thinking and training does go into it, no doubt. On stage, however, what we see is not the effort but the absorption of the dancer in the dance. Almost as a counterpoint, on my first reading of her poetry, I felt that while the poetic form and technique seem uncomplicated, the poetic thoughts contained in them are complex and reveal a deep study of, reflection upon and immersion in profound spiritual wisdom.

The poetry may come to her spontaneously, but her mind has been prepared to receive that poetry and transmit it in words by years of close engagement with the best thoughts from some of the best minds, especially in the Indian spiritual tradition; and these provide apt epigraphs to every one of her poems. The reader is all the richer for gaining access to these poets through Harinie's poetry. As a dancer, she has interpreted the thoughts of creative minds as diverse as Adi Shankara, Thirumoolar, Tagore, Lal Ded and Annamacharya. Living with their words and their intuitive perception, and embodying their rhythms in her dance every single day has made it possible for Harinie to internalise them, make them her own and form them forth afresh in newer expressions. It is ancient wisdom that Harinie speaks of in these poems, although in an idiom all her own. Like the guru-parampara one invokes in the spiritual tradition, here is a kavi-parampara that is made available to us readers in this aesthetic tradition.

The division of the poems into Jnana, Karma and Bhakti is, Harinie says, happenstance. But then, the progression seems so natural, so much of an intuitive design. The movement from the meditative, reflective Jnana through the slightly fast-paced but still self-aware path of Karma, to the ecstatic self oblivion of Bhakti is seamless. Harinie moves effortlessly from the casually playful andhaadhi to the apprehension of beauty "in this carefully scripted play". The "Elemental Cries" shatter the "Writer's Block" leading her on to the Emersonian Karmabhoomi (Field of Action) and Rangabhoomi (Field of War/ Theatre). All this frenetic activity is then sweetly harmonised in the Self merging in the Shiva/Vishnu Tattva. Particularly stunning is Harinie's interpretation of the Narasimha avatara, which visualises "the unhurrying chase and the unperturbed pace" of the Lord running to do his devotee's bidding, brooking no delay.

The verbal art of Harinie's poetry is complemented by the visual art of Kum. Meghna Unnikrishnan. The black and white sketches foreground the patterns woven into the poems. They capture the energy and the inscape of Harinie's imagination. The sketches are not merely illustrations of the poems; they are creative visualisations; they are co-texts bearing their own meanings and thought patterns, running parallel to and enriching the words on the page. The artwork for the poem "End & Beginnining: Andhaadhi" re-creates the structural pattern of the poem; the fluidity and continuity is marked by repeating the last pattern of each panel as the first pattern of the succeeding panel. This is a re-creation of the poetic vision into an artistic vision indeed! Meghna's artwork reminds us readers again that art is a single, fluid, unifying experience, though the media of expression may differ.

I have listened to my Guru explain Jnana, Karma and Bhakti thus: Jnana is knowing how to make a sweet dish, Karma is actually making it and Bhakti is tasting the flavor—the rasaanubhava—of the sweet dish. May Chidambaresa, the Dancing Lord, continue to bless Harinie and Meghna with an integrated experience of all three modes! And may we continue to be Celebrants at the Feast of their visual and verbal poetry on stage and on page!

K. Latha

Assistant Professor,

Department of English,

Stella Maris College, Chennai

PREFACE

'...It is a fastidious old friend,
It comes only when it comes.

Like the heavy clouds that hold up
And burst open all of a sudden,
It will happen one day. Until then,
The parchment and quill will have to stay.'

Like a guest who arrives unannounced at your doorstep, enters your house, stays for a brief period of time, and during that stay makes you forget the world, at the end of it all, makes you feel you are the guest and they, the host. That's all there is to be said; nothing more.

I am not a habitual writer. Therefore, I consider my brief, unexpected encounters with writing—special. The poems happen sometimes in the busiest streets and sometimes in the middle of a night's deep sleep, mostly to be forgotten the next morning. Out of all the pieces of writing that have happened so far, this one has taken the longest to arrive—this Preface—I have waited for months for the right words, because there is a lot to be said and many to be left unsaid.

This anthology is a collection of some poems that have happened over the last few years. These poems are neither meant to be outright proclamations nor any aphorisms. These are mere perspectives that may come, evolve and go.

The Universe has its way of speaking to us—through silent yet strong signals. During the last one year, as I was reading English translations of Indian literary works, I got some approving nods and some curt Nos from them—Tagore, Kabir, Bhartrhari, Bharathi and many more. The verses that are preludes to each of the poems in this anthology are a result of the last one year's search—like an assuring smile to the vein of a leaf from the banyan tree.

While the hunt for verses gave depth to my experience, reflecting on visual representations for the poems added dimension. Young, committed, hard working, full of zest—patiently waiting alongside me when I waited for the muses to throw visuals upon me; patiently listening to the visualisations; patiently showing me draft after draft; patiently travelling with me through this journey with silent excitement—Meghna Unnikrishnan has, in a way, become the anchor to this ship.

I owe my heartfelt gratitude to many for their selfless contribution in terms of time and knowledge to make this happen. My parents top the list for always quietly letting me be in my world of perspectives. I am grateful to Latha ma'am for reading the manuscript, giving suggestions and graciously agreeing to write the Foreword. My sincere thanks to Kishore Anna, an exemplary artiste and in this context, a Literature enthusiast, for playing the devil's advocate (sometimes, a rather severe one!) for my choice of verses and illustrations. I owe a huge thanks to Ms. Avanti Natarajan (The Art Brew Creative Company), the designer of this book, for her professional and meticulous work, taking personal interest and always making me feel that the book was in safe hands. To Gowri Ravindranath aunty and Ravindranath uncle, I convey my thanks, for giving me the first nudge of confidence to publish my works and being silent onlookers of this process.

To all my Teachers—human, incidental, natural—for they mould me, make me question and seek—I pay my obeisance.

My perspectives are laid bare here. You, my reader, may read them and interpret as your perspectives lead. The poems are ready; the poetry is yet to begin.

Let the reading commence,
And I,
I shall wait for the guest
To knock at my door,
Again once...

Perspectives—thus, the world.

Harinie Jeevitha

JNĀNA MĀRGAM
THE PATH OF WISDOM

...मायाकल्पितदेशकालकलना वैचित्र्यचित्रीकृतम्
मायावीव विजृम्भयत्यपि महायोगीव यः स्वेच्छया...
(दक्षिणामूर्ति स्तोत्रम्, आदि शङ्कराचार्य)

...māyākalpitadēśakālakalanā vaicitryacitrīkṛtam
māyāvīva vijṛmbhayatyapi mahāyōgīva yaḥ svēcchayā...
(Dakśhiṇāmūrti Stōtram, Adi Shankaracharya)

Like a magician, who fabricates various pictures
of time and space by the illusory capacity,
The great yogi too, manifests the universe, with His very own will.

∴

THE ARTIST'S SKETCH

The Universe is a painting.
Each stroke–a perspective.
The Universe I see is not the same as yours,
For the Reds and Blues are unique
To each pair of eyes.

We marvel at the painting;
Interpretations millions we give.
But only the Artist knows
What each stroke means
Or maybe He doesn't!

Nevertheless,
He is the artist,
he **Is** the artist,
he is **The** artist,
he is the **Artist** who painted it all...

The painting is ephemeral yet eternal.
It is a mirage, a reflection, an illusion,
Yet it seems so real, so now and palpable.
Some clean strokes, some clumsy ones too;

Nevertheless,
He is the artist,
he **Is** the artist,
he is **The** artist,
he is the **Artist** who painted it all...

∴

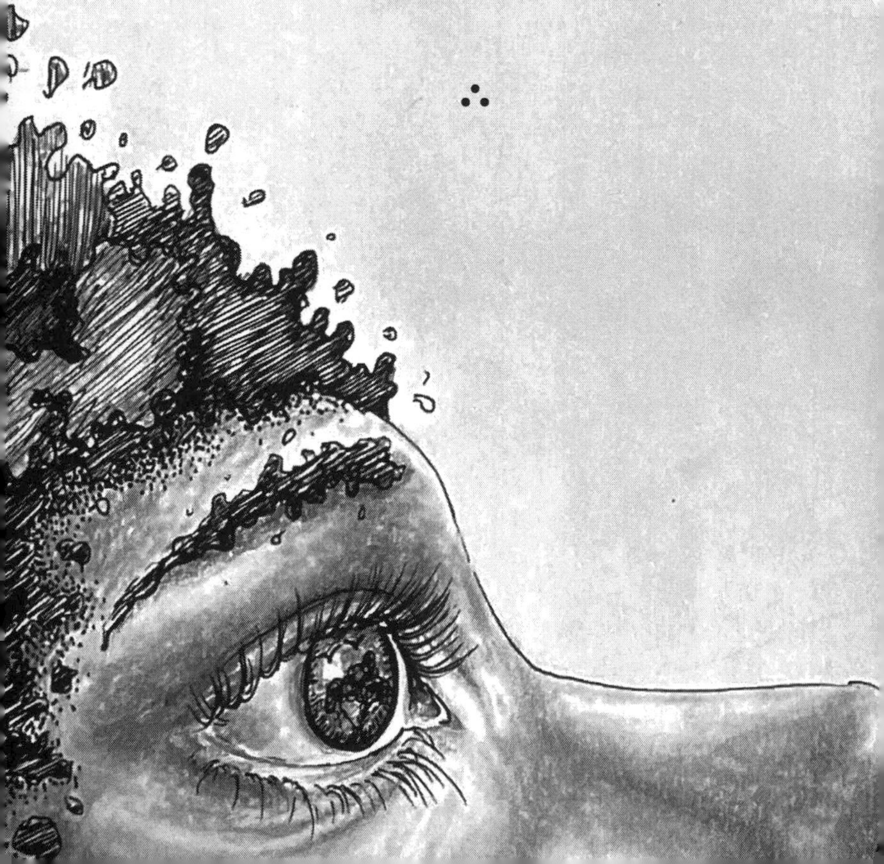

पर् त पान् यॅम्य सॊमुय् मोन
यॅम्य हिहुय् मोन् द्यन् क्योह राथ् ।
यमिसय् अद्वय मन् सॉम्पुन्
तॅमिय् ड्यूठुय् सुरगुरुनाथ् ॥
(लाल् देद्)

par ta pān ye'mya so'mŭy mŏn
ye'mya hihuy mŏn dyan kyoha rāth ǀ
ye'misŭy advai man sămpŭn,
tamiy dyūṭhuy sŭragurunāth ǁ
(Lal Ded)

Who accepts oneself and other as the same,
Who understands that day and night are the same–
That one's mind has become non-dual;
That very person has perceived the God of gods.

∴

DUALITY

Standing in a solitary garden,
Staring at a pile of green grass,
She and I exchanged looks of dismay.
What she saw, I did not see.

Leaning on the wet shore
With sand caressing our hair,
She saw the unending sky aghast
But I sensed the echoing waves.

She showed me the perched birds,
I did see them, but not like hers.
She showed me the surreal sunset,
That I did see, but hardly like hers.

Carried away by the scenic beauty,
Every detail did we try to see.
Every moment did we try to live.
But no two moments matched.

Stepping to where I had stood,
She looked around.
Placing my feet where she earlier had,
I looked around too.

For we saw two different worlds,
Worlds that never collided with one another,
For however similar they seemed,
However alike we thought them to be.

They were two unlike worlds,
Fragments of imagination they were,
Perspectives of a painting they were,
Dregs of our inundating Dreams.

If the worlds we saw were the same,
There would be neither sorrow nor joy,
Neither greed nor selflessness,
Neither war nor love.

Behold! There would be neither 'She'
Nor any 'I'.

∴

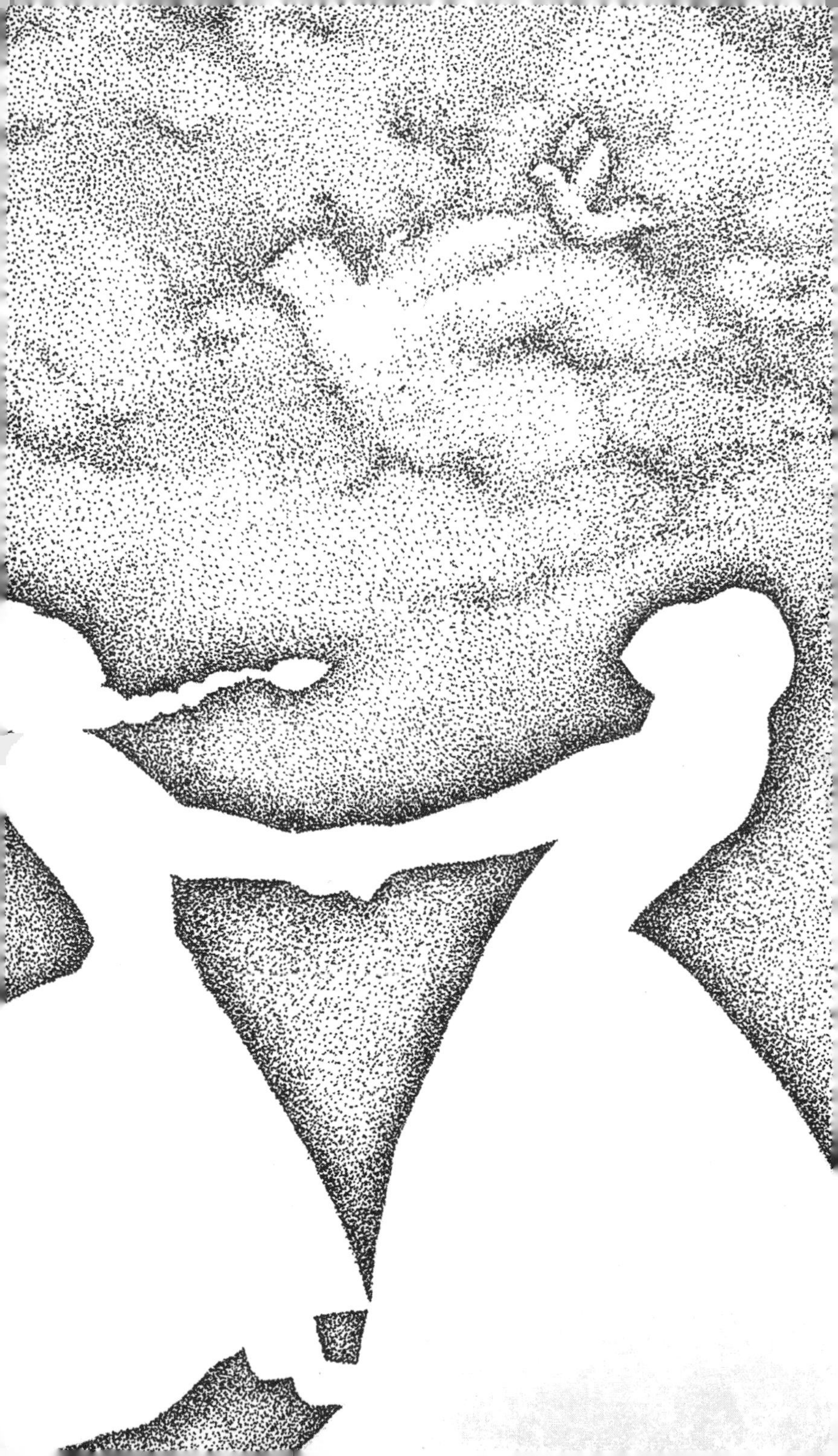

நில்லாத வற்றை நிலையின என்றுணரும்
புல்லறி வாண்மை கடை.
(திருக்குறள், திருவள்ளுவர்)

nillādha vaṟṟai nilaiyiṇa eṇṟuṉarum
pullaṟi vāṉmai kadai.
(Thirukkuṟaḻ, Thiruvalluvar)

A disgrace to mankind it is, that ignorant mind,
which thinks of the
fleeting impermanent as a constant permanent.

∴

THIS TOO SHALL PASS

This too shall pass, this too shall pass
Like the stirring waves of the stringent sea.
Before one wave touches the shore,
The other approaches.
The sea sucks them all
To begin all over again.

This too shall pass, this too shall pass
Like the sun that rises
When the world is asleep,
And sets secretively
When one hardly cares.
It goes on and on, again and again.

This too shall pass, this too shall pass
Like the myriad of expressions
On the face of the thespian.

When one Act is over,
It evaporates in thin air.
In another Act, a new expression is born.

This too shall pass, this too shall pass.
There are no constants, alas!
Sorrow, joy, fear, anger: juvenile germs
That will be soon lost.

Tomorrow, a new sorrow and joy
Will be born.
But, that too will pass.

∴

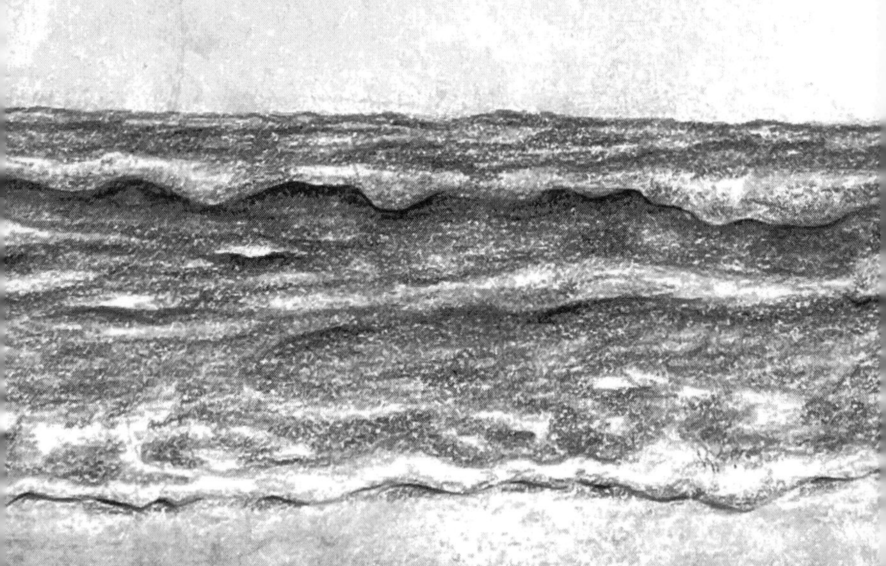

मनस्येकं वचस्येकं कर्मण्येकं महात्मनाम् ।
मनस्यन्यद्वचस्यन्यत् कार्येचान्यद्दुरात्मनाम् ॥
(समयोचित पद्यमालिका)

manasyēkaṃ vacasyēkaṃ karmaṇyēkaṃ mahātmanām ।
manasyanyadvacasyanyat kāryēcānyaddurātmanām ॥
(Samayōcita Padyamālikā)

Noble is the one whose thought, word and action are one.
Wicked is the one whose thought is one,
word is one other and action is one another.

∴

TRIPURA: HAYWIRE

There were three powerful demons
Who guised as cities.
One was unconquerable—thoughts,
The second was a trickster—words,
And the third, an agitated one—actions.

They revolved and revolved,
Yet never met on the same plane.
Each city took pride in its worth,
One was made of precious gold,
The second was of silver,
And the third was iron that soon became old.

Astray were their strides;
Never once in line.
Seeing their pitiable plight,
The celestials took flight.
Oh! What havoc the three cities caused–
Being never once aligned.

The four scriptures galloped to them,
Sun and Moon rolled unto their aid.
The Earth charioted towards them;
The mighty mountain bowed.
But of what use were these,
Until He laughed aloud!

He used no bow and arrow,
He knew His work was done.
They became ashes and merged in Him.
For, when the three cities–
Thoughts, Words and Actions aligned,
That was the moment of Liberation.

∴

மரத்தை மறைத்தது மாமத யானை
மரத்தின் மறைந்தது மாமத யானை
பரத்தை மறைத்தது பார் முதல் பூதம்
பரத்தின் மறைந்தது பார் முதல் பூதமே.
(திருமந்திரம், திருமூலர்)

maraththai maṟaiththadhu māmadha yāṇai
maraththiṇ maṟaindhadhu māmadha yāṇai
paraththai maṟaiththadhu pār mudhal būdham
paraththiṇ maṟaindhadhu pār mudhal būdhamē.
(Thirumandhiram, Thirumoolar)

The mighty elephant hid the wood, of which it is made;
(Nay) The wood, in fact, hid the mighty elephant.
Universe hid the Supreme, of which it is made,
(Nay) It is the Supreme which hid the Universe in Him.

∴

EACH & EVERY

The cosmos is smeared by thy presence,
Thou art the atoms strewn everywhere,
It is thine self that wriggles, walks and flies,
Yet we let be, ourselves, lost in the lies.

We count not the number of leaves,
For the tree is full of them.
We care not for the buzz of each bee,
For the hive is full of them.

We know not the fragrance
Of every fallen Autumn flower,
We mind not the taste
Of every grain of cooking flour.

We feel not the gentle slap of sunshine
On our hardened cheeks.
In Each and Every thing—Thou art,
What a fallacy! We vividly see, yet we don't.

Things that are in abundance,
We care not for their existence.
The cosmos is smeared by thy presence,
Seldom do we imbibe that essence.

এ আমার শরীরের শিরায় শিরায়
যে প্রাণ—তরঙ্গমালা রাত্রিদিন ধায়
সেই প্রাণ অপরূপ ছন্দে তালে লয়ে
নাচিছে ভুবনে...
(গীতাঞ্জলি, রবীন্দ্রনাথ ঠাকুর)

e āmār śarīrer śirāẏ śirāẏ
je prān—taraṅgamālā rātridin dhāẏ
sei prān aparūp chande tāle laẏe
nāciche bhubane...
(Gitāñjali, Rabindranath Tagore)

In each vein of my body,
Life runs like a garland of waves, night and day;
That same life resonates in rhythm, meter and speed,
And dances in this Universe...

∴

WHERE DO I BELONG?

If my head is the infinite skies,
And my body, the widespread land,
Afloat in mid space I dwell.
Where do I live? Where do I belong?

The vast oceans call me unto them,
The winds remind me of a forgotten past,
With passion they call out to me.
Where do I live? Where do I belong?

The trees stare a stoic glance,
The leaves whisper in my ears,
They invite me to join them.
Where do I live? Where do I belong?

The sands tickle and clasp my feet,
Pleading me to stay with them,
Insects pen messages on my skin,
So that I, for a bit, remember them.

The wink of the stars,
The touch of the rain,
The fragrance of a flower,
The sound of a nearby stream–
So familiar they all seem.

If my head is the infinite skies,
And my body, the widespread land,
Afloat in mid space I dwell.
Where do I live? Where do I belong?

∴

भान गॊल तॉय् प्रकाश् आव् ज़ूने
ॖचन्दर गॊल तॉय् मॊतय ॖच्यथ् ।
ॖचयथ् गॊल तॉय् कैंह् ति ना कुने
गयि भूर् भुवः स्वर् मीलिथ् कोत ॥
(लाल् देद्)

bhān go'l tay prakāś āv zūne
tçandŭr go'l tay mo'tuy tçayth ।
tçyath go'l tay keinh ti nā kune
gayi bhūr bhuvaḥ svar mīlith kot ॥
(Lal Ded)

When the sun dissolves, the moonlight remains;
When the moon phases dissolve, the mind alone remains;
When the mind dissolves, nothing remains.
Earth, ether and sky depart.

∴

MIRROR

She created the sky
And its drifting clouds.
She created the sea
And its pounding waves.
She created the land
And innumerable grains of sand.
She created the fire
And its agitated sparks.
She created the winds
In its ceaseless form.
She created them all
To resemble the mind–
With
drifting,
        pounding,
i n n u m e r a b l e,
a   g   i
      t   a
  t   e d,
ceaseless thoughts.

She made the cosmos

A mirror–

A mirror to the mind

That harbours a million thoughts.

Each grows in the company

Of the other—mind and mirror.

When one ceases to exist,

The other departs.

ఎరుగువా రెరుగుదు రీయర్ధము
యెరగని వారికి ఇది యెరగనీయ్యదు.
మొదల గలుగువాడే ముందరను గలవాడు
అదన నాతడే పరమాత్ముడు
యెదుట గలిగినదే ఇన్నిటా గలిగినది
పదపడి యిదియే ప్రపంచము.
(అన్నమాచార్య)

eruguvā rerugudu rīyardhamu
yeragani vāriki idi yeraganīyadu.
modala galuguvāḍē mundaranu galavāḍu
adana nātaḍē paramātmuḍu
yeduṭa galiginadē innitā galiginadi
padapaḍi yidiyē prapañcamu.
(Annamacharya)

Those who know what this means, will know.
Those who do not know, will not.
The one, who is in the beginning, will also be in the end;
He is verily the Supreme.
What is in front of you is everywhere;
This alone, we call the universe.

∴

END & BEGINNING: ANDHĀDHI

Different are the things we see,
Yet arising from the same speck they be.
Varied in form and colour they seem,
But only to eyes that just **see.**

See ahead of what surrounds,
No looming trees or big seas.
Just simple specks sewn along
An invisible thread long and **strong.**

Strong is the sameness between two specks.
Haven't you sensed that all along?
Ears would hear it when kept shut
And eyes would see when **closed.**

Closed in specks tightly, it be.
Yet so open for the world to see.
Beginning and end of the poem–

The world—it be.

So same they seem. None any **different.**

Andhādhi is a genre of Tamil poetry where the last word of a verse becomes the first word of the next verse. The last word of the series of verses is also the first word of the very first verse.

∴

KARMA MĀRGAM
THE PATH OF DUTY

यतः प्रवृत्तिर्भूतानां येन सर्वमिदं ततम् ।
स्वकर्मणा तमभ्यर्च्य सिद्धिं विन्दति मानवः ॥
(श्रीमद्भगवद्गीता, व्यास मुनि)

yataḥ pravṛttirbhūtānāṃ yēna sarvamidaṃ tatam I
svakarmaṇā tamabhyarcya siddhiṃ vindati mānavaḥ II
(Śrīmadbhagavadgītā, Vyasa muni)

From whom beings originate; by whom this entirety is pervaded:
With one's own duty, Him, when worshipped, man attains perfection.

∴

POLICEMAN AND THE THIEF

Once there lived a policeman,
Who was respected by every townsman.
A strong, brave policeman was he,
Too proud of his good deeds indeed!

Sometimes he boasted to himself,
Sometimes he acted humble,
Sometimes he whined about his job,
Sometimes he rejoiced in its rewards.

Nevertheless, he was a policeman,
A good policeman indeed!

Once there lived a thief,
A thief who stole passionately.
He stole every other day,
A rupee or a hundred,
Whatever came his way.

He was true to his job,
That even when hit by a mob
He never gave up on it.
So true he was to his job,
That slowly he saw God in it.

"O dear, steal not! In this business,
You deal not!" God said.
The God of Stealth showed–
The real wealth to him and left.

Awakened from his slumber,
The thief, who was asleep, sat up.
He sat with his eyes shut,
Dark outside, but insides lit up.

It is the truth of the thief to steal,
And that of the police to protect.
What one's truth is doesn't matter,
For the 'truthness' in it will take you
To Truth's very own Altar.

∴

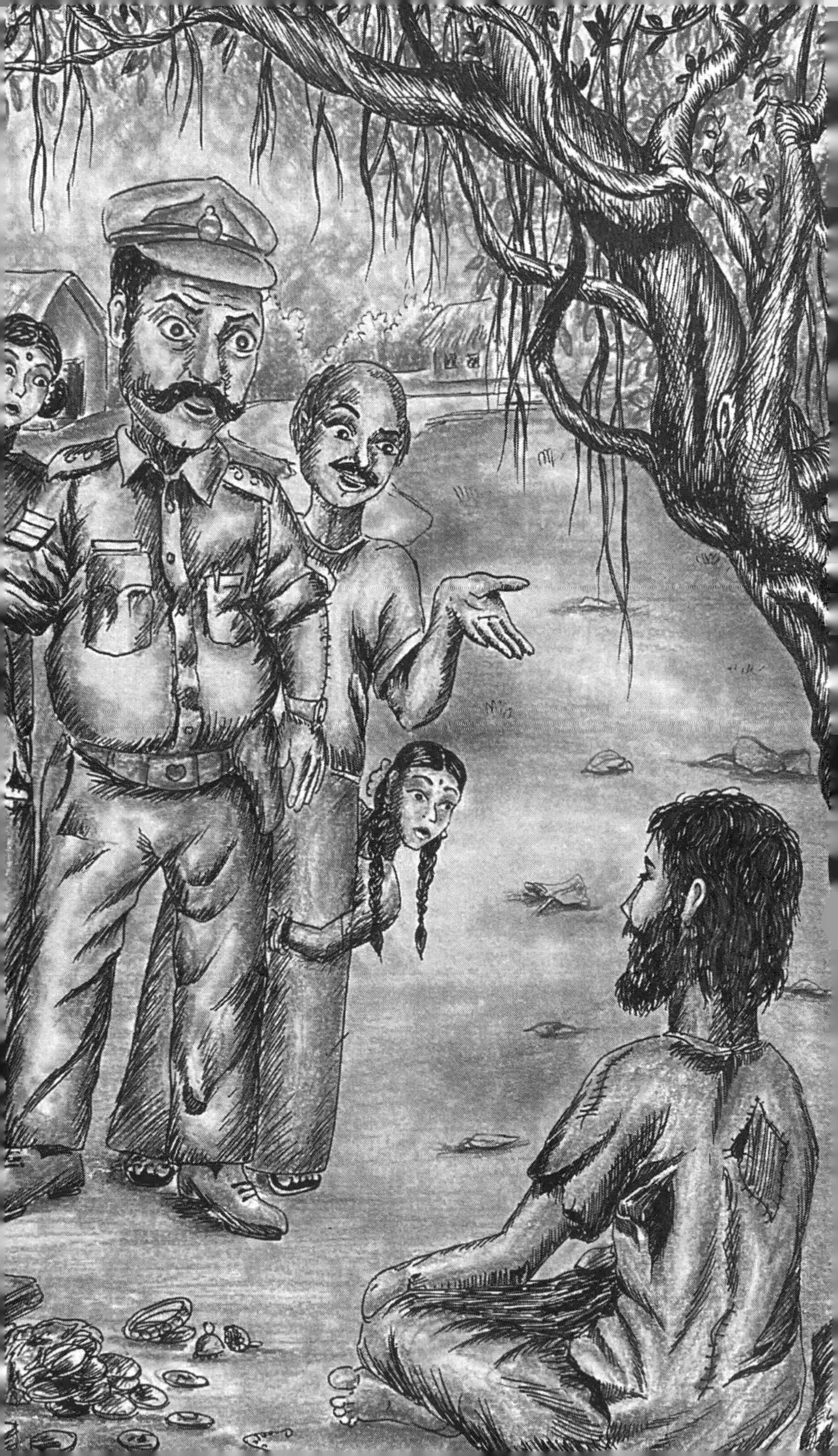

...உடலென்ற கும்பிக்கு உணவென்ற விரைத்தேடி
ஓயாமல் இரவுபகலும்
உண்டுண்டு உறங்குவதைக் கண்டதே அல்லாமல்
ஒரு பயனடைந்திலேனை...
(நடராஜ பத்து, சிறுமணவூர் முனுசாமி)

...udaleṇṟa kumbikku uṉaveṇṟa viraiththēdi
ōyāmal iravupagalum
uṉduṉdu uṟaṅguvadhaik kaṉdadhē allāmal
oru payaṇadaindhilēṇai...
(Natarāja Paththu, Sirumanavoor Munusami)

...For the body that is sheer appetite,
tirelessly hunting day and night for a prey that is food;
Other than eating and sleeping,
I have achieved no purpose at all...

∴

TIME TRAVEL

Amidst the tensed towns of
Past, Present and Future,
Where exactly, do I reside?
At times, amazed by the
Antiquity of Past,
Sometimes, satisfied with the
Serendipity of Present,
Otherwise carried away by the
Aroma of Future,
This tiring travel I make with Time,
In search of a speck of grain
From a pile of sand.

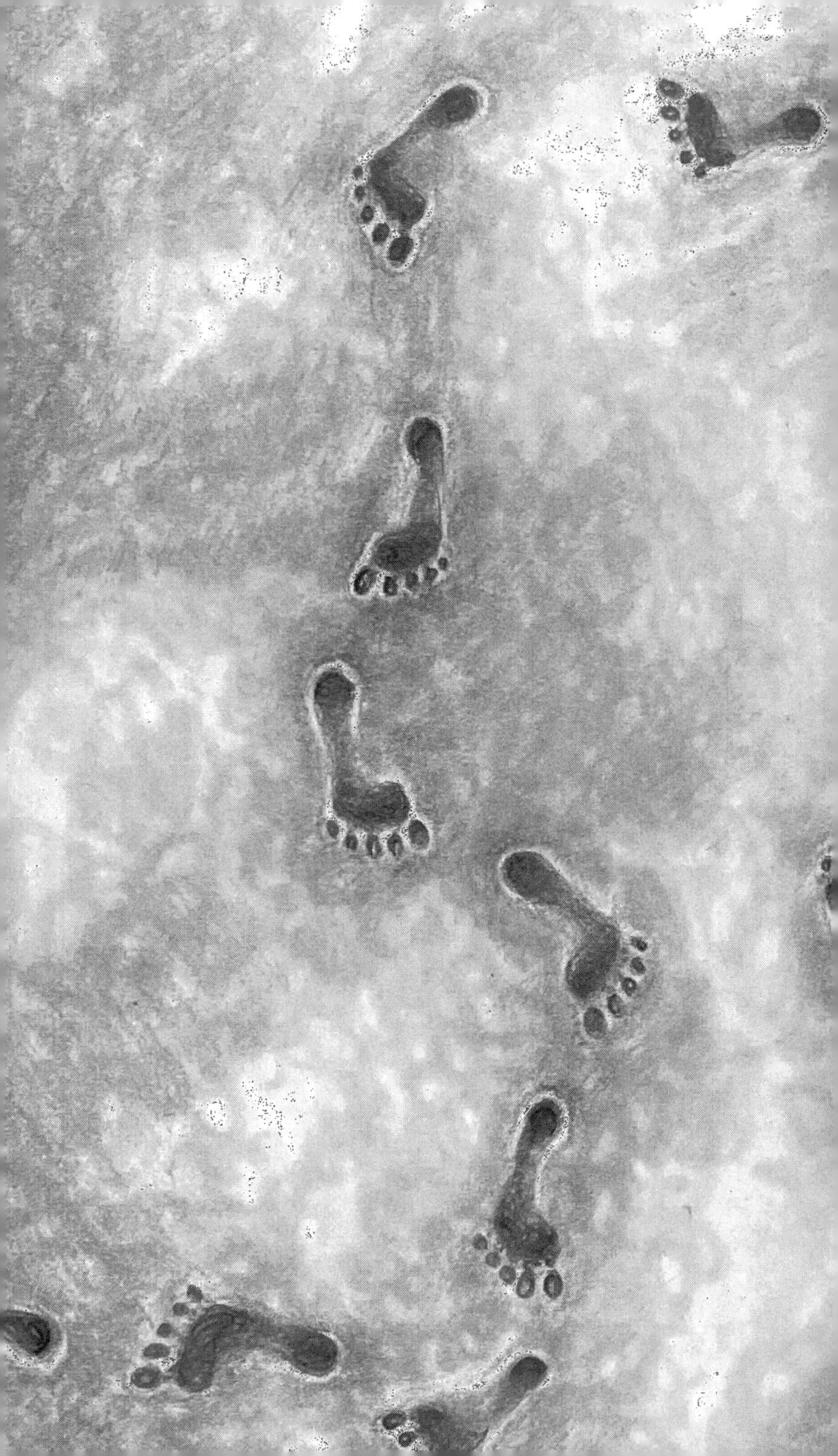

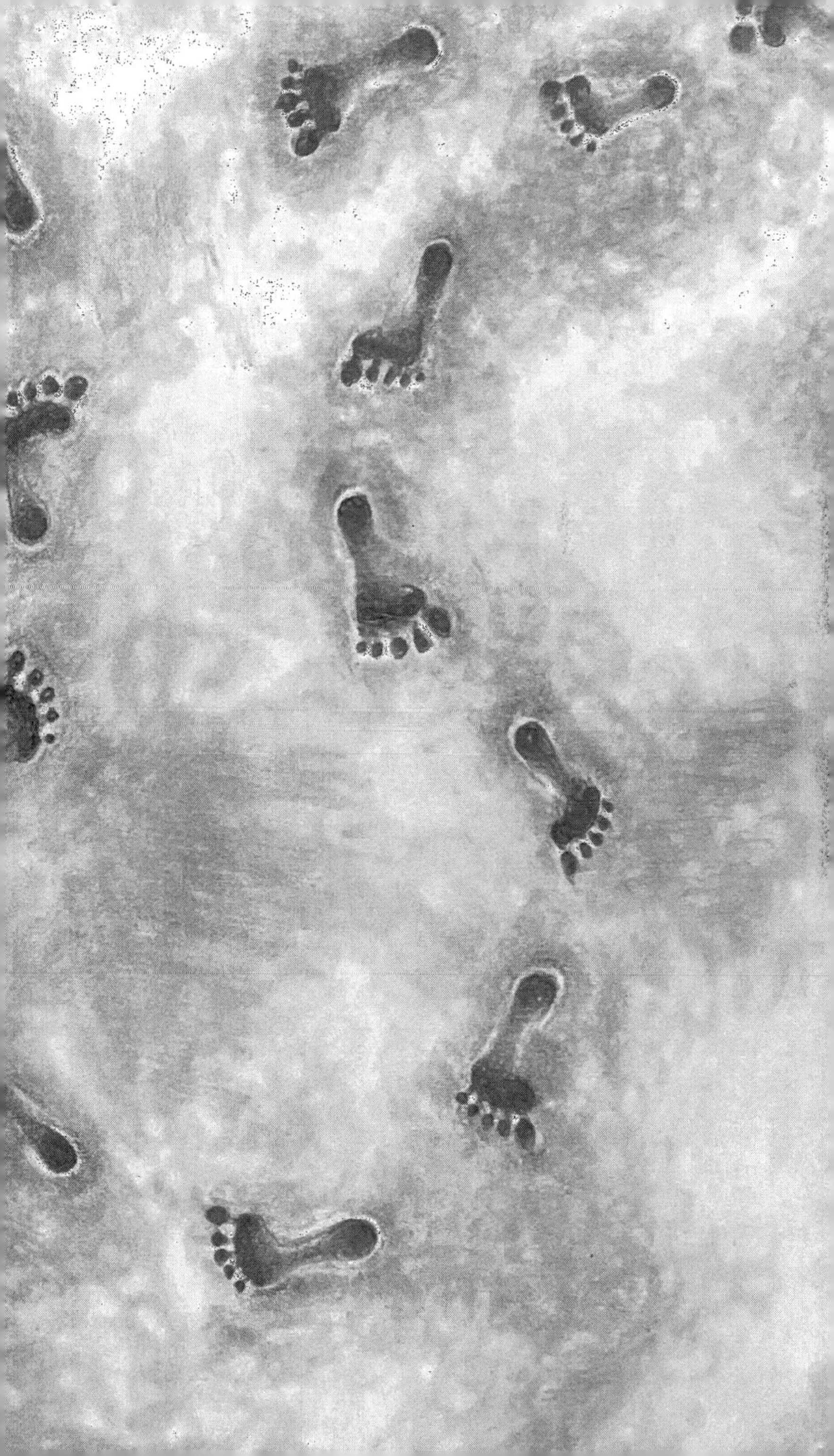

పుట్టుటయు నిజము పోవుటయు నిజము
నట్ట నడిమీ పని నాటకము...
తెగదు పాపము తీరదు పుణ్యము
నగి నగి కాలము నాటకము...
నానాటి బ్రతుకు నాటకము...
(అన్నమాచార్య)

puṭṭuṭayu nijamu pōvuṭayu nijamu
naṭṭa naḍimī pani nāṭakamu...
tegadu pāpamu tīradu puṇyamu
nagi nagi kālamu nāṭakamu...
nānāṭi bratuku nāṭakamu...
(Annamacharya)

To be born is truth; to die is truth too;
Chores in between is Drama...
The sins do not snap; Puṇyam never ends;
This farcical Time is Drama...
Everyday life is sheer Drama...

∴

ACT 1, SCENE 5

That which triggers a smile or a tear,
Each move that kindles envy or fear,
Every drop of rain or ray of sunshine,
Places full of light or lulled in darkness,
Among all that there is,
None can be bereft of beauty.

Beauty is what is around
In this carefully scripted play.
A play—unrehearsed, spontaneous, gripping;
A play which He merrily directs,
And we amateur artistes merely act.

∴

विहतामिव च श्रद्धाम् आशां प्रतिहतामिव ।
सोपसर्गां यथा सिद्धिं बुद्धिं सकलुषामिव ॥
(वाल्मीकि रामायणं, वाल्मीकि मुनि)

vihatāmiva ca śraddhām āśāṃ pratihatāmiva I
sōpasargāṃ yathā siddhiṃ buddhiṃ sakaluṣāmiva II
(Vālmīki Rāmāyaṇaṃ, Valmiki muni)

(Sita appeared) Like faith that is shattered; like hope that is let down;
Like success that is obstructed; like intellect that is impaired.

∴

ELEMENTAL CRIES

When his greedy hands pierced through the ground and he let out his lecherous laughter, Mother **Earth** shuddered in anger and promised to engulf me into Her womb from which I emerged.

As he took me in a bird-like chariot, the birds beside froze in their flight, perplexed at the sight. The helpless **Sky** closed its eyes in shame and shed tears desperately, ceaselessly.

He vehemently drove past the **Sea** with lustful eyes. On hearing my screams, the sullen sea surged upwards to reach out to me, splashing its arms unto me, to take me back to the serpent bed, where I belong.

The **Winds** shook their heads in disapproval of the disaster. Chasing the chariot closely, they brought with them a message from their leader. His son would come to my rescue, they said and left.

The **earth** shook; the **spaces** shuddered, **seas** shivered, **winds** howled. Didn't He, the controller of the five elements, understand their cries?

Oh, there was one element left behind: **Fire.** He waited for the final cry from that Sire.

∴

வாராய்! கவிதையாம் மணிபெயர்க் காதலி!
பன்னாள் பன்மதி ஆண்டுபல கழிந்தன,
நின்னருள் வதனம்நான் நேருறக் கண்டே...
(சுப்பிரமணிய பாரதி)

vārāi kavidhaiyām man̠ipeyark kādhali!
paṇṇāl̠ paṇmadhi ān̠dupala kazhindhaṇa,
niṇṇarul̠ vadhaṇamnāṇ nērur̠ak kan̠dē...
(Subramanya Bharathi)

Come, O Poesy, my beloved!
Many days, many months, many years have passed,
Since I beheld your compassionate face...

∴

WRITER'S BLOCK

The lightning has hit,
And the thunder growls,
The sky is a sheepish shade
Of placid mauve.

The leaves drip with water,
Rooftops sing pitter-patter,
In the secretive silence that gently loads,
The showers bend and kiss the roads.

Spreading bare a parchment,
Finger gaps tickled by the quill,
Envying the sands and skies,
I wait for it to come.

Senses fed, heart a-full,
Now is when it will come.
I wait and wait, nibbling the quill,
For the parchment, in words, to fill.

It yields not to my codswallop cries,
It comes only when it comes.
It is a fastidious, old friend,
It comes only when it comes.

Like the heavy clouds that hold up,
And burst open all of a sudden,
It will happen one day. Until then,
The parchment and quill will have to stay.

∴

अहमात्मा गुडाकेश सर्वभूताशयस्थितः ।
अहमादिश्च मध्यं च भूतानामन्त एव च ॥
(श्रीमद्भगवद्गीता, व्यास मुनि)

ahamātmā guḍākēśa sarvabhūtāśayasthitaḥ |
ahamādiśca madhyaṃ ca bhūtānāmanta ēva ca ||
(Śrīmadbhagavadgītā, Vyasa muni)

I am the Self seated in the heart of all beings,
O conqueror of sleep (Arjuna)!
I am the beginning and middle of beings; and their end too.

∴

WAR FIELD

Go, Arjuna! Do not hesitate!
Fight them all! Do not hesitate!
They are your kith and kin, I know,
You have grown up with them, I know.
Anger, desire, envy, greed, pride–
Your kith and kin, indeed.
It could be hard to part with them,
But go, Arjuna, fight them all!
Don't shudder at the sight of
The battlefield filled with dead bodies:
They are your thoughts of the past.
Don't shiver at the sight of
The warriors who approach with weapons:
They are your fears of the future.
Trust in me, ho Arjuna!
For, I can sail you through this war.
Trust in me, ho Arjuna!
For, I am the lone fighter and the fought.

...बेद बड़ा कि जहां तैं आया?
यहु मन बड़ा कि जेहिं मन मांनौं?
राम बड़ा कि रामहिं जांनैं?
(संत कबीर)

...bēd baḍā ki jahāñ tain āyā?
yahu man baḍā ki jēhiñ man mānaun?
rām baḍā ki rāmhin jānain?
(Sant Kabir)

...Is Vēda greater or its source?
Is the mind greater or what it thinks?
Is Lord Ram greater or the one who surrenders to Him?

∴

THE GREATER ODE

Is there a greater compassion than
Simply forgiving?
Is there a greater discipline than
Watching your thoughts?
Is there a greater prayer than
Wishing for peace?
Is there a greater ritual than
Acknowledging the divine in all?

Is there a greater charity than
Giving unending love?
Is there a greater penance than
Being in the present?
Is there a greater victory than
Winning over anger?
Is there a greater happiness than
Seeing beauty in all?

Is there a greater strength than
Being weightless?
Is there a greater love than
The selfless mother's?
Is there a greater duty than
Cleansing the mind?
Is there a greater affirmation than
A smile and a nod?

Is there a greater humility than
Complete surrender to the Lord?
Is there a greater knowledge than
Knowing no error was intentional at all?
Is there a greater freedom than
Being with yourself at any cost?
Is there a greater wisdom than
Realising that this too shall pass?

கண்ணன் மாளிகைக்கே வந்தேனோ
கண்கட்டு வித்தை இதுவோ!

அமலன் விமலன் கண்ணன் திருசேவைக்கு பின்பு
சித்தப்ரஹ்மம்கொண்டு சுற்றி சுற்றி வழி தெரியாமல்

கண்ணன் மாளிகைக்கே வந்தேனோ!
(பாபநாசம் சிவன்)

kaṉṉaṇ māḻigaikkē vandhēṇō
kaṉkattu viththai idhuvō!

amalaṇ vimalaṇ kaṉṉaṇ thirusēvaikku piṇbu
chiththabrahmamkoṉdu churṟi churṟi vazhi theriyāmal

kaṉṉaṇ māḻigaikkē vandhēṇō!
(Papanasam Sivan)

Have I come back to Kannan's palace?
What is this illusory game!

After the company of the faultless one, who makes us pure,
In intoxication, treading around, not knowing the path–

Have I come back to Kannan's palace?

∴

INTENTION: AN EPIC POEM

For days together, He had been planning
For the arrival of His friend.
Servants were forbidden from cleaning
The palace; fine dust on tables, patches on
Mirrors—are just what He wanted.
Shining shawls replaced with sombre ones,
Glistening furniture sent to godowns.
Erasing each trace of flamboyance,
He carefully prepared for the
Unannounced arrival of His friend.
Like a frail trace of a frivolous flash back,
Bent with the weight of poverty,
His friend walked miles and miles
With barely any footwear
To give him good company.
Krishna walked restlessly in His gardens–
He removed His footwear, left His chest bare.
Amidst the pricks of thorns, bites of winds,
Awaiting eagerly:

The unannounced arrival of His friend.
The palace gates opened
To half-heartedly welcome the entrant,
Who seemed like an ounce of unasked air
In a rich garden—like a poor contestant.
Like the first drop of rain
The parched land gets,
Like the first vision
The blind gets to see,
Like the child that runs to its mother
After being lost in a crowd,
Sudhama felt.
Krishna made the first move:
He ran, He hugged;
The frail figure shrinking further
In the warmth of His majestic arms.
Who hid their tears more?
The answers were in their palms.
He took him into the palace,
Showed him off to His guards,
Introduced him to His wives
As the noblest friend from His past.

Krishna recalled their childhood days;
Sudhama's worries had dulled his memory.
The master script writer spun new stories
Just for the smile on the face of His friend.
Sudhama never lied to Krishna,
Until that day when he said "Yes",
When asked if all was well.
Sudhama's momentary happiness
Became the cause for his added guilt;
He was rejoicing in Krishna's presence
While his family suffered in silence,
With barely any food or quilt.
"Have you brought me any butter, Sudhama?
Have you brought me some wet sand
From Mathura, O Sudhama?
Or have you any letters from our friends?
What have you brought for me, Sudhama?",
Krishna said.
If Guilt ever felt guilty, if Sorrow ever felt sad,
If Pain had ever felt hurt:
That is all what Sudhama felt.
Clutching the knot of his shrunken Dhoti,

Vehemently shaking his head,
Sudhama lied again–
"No, Krishna. I have nothing for you",
He said.
"I have stolen pots of butter from roofs atop,
My friend; I have snatched jars of milk too.
What big task would it be to grasp
The bundle that you so tightly clasp!
Loosen the grip; the bundle is mine",
He said.
Krishna and His wives relished
Every bit of the beaten rice
As Sudhama stood in a fix.
Sudhama ran out of the chambers,
And out of the palace,
Never once looking back.
Reminded of his wife and children,
Eyes blurred with guilty tears,
Satiated by Krishna's company
He ran and ran until he swooned
With tiredness and shock
On the marble stair of a looming block.

In the grainy sight that Sudhama saw,
Stood his wife and children, in riches; in awe.

Krishna is the Universe,
Sudhama is the intention.
The Universe has its way
Of answering them all.

BHAKTI MĀRGAM
THE PATH OF DEVOTION

शिवाय विष्णुरूपाय शिवरूपाय विष्णवे ।
शिवस्य हृदयं विष्णुः विष्णोश्च हृदयं शिवः ॥
यथा शिवमयो विष्णुः एवं विष्णुमयः शिवः ।
यथान्तरं नपश्यामि तथामे स्वस्तिरायुषि ॥
(यजुर्वेद)

śivāya viṣṇurūpāya śivarūpāya viṣṇavē I
śivasya hṛdayaṃ viṣṇuḥ viṣṇōśca hṛdayaṃ śivaḥ II
yathā śivamayō viṣṇuḥ ēvaṃ viṣṇumayaḥ śivaḥ I
yathāntaraṃ napaśyāmi tathāmē svastirāyuṣi II
(Yajurvēda)

For Shiva, form is Vishnu; Vishnu's form is Shiva;
Shiva's heart is Vishnu and Vishnu's heart is Shiva.
Where Shiva has pervaded, there is Vishnu;
Where Vishnu has pervaded, there is only Shiva,
As I do not perceive the difference between the two,
so may my life prosper.

∴

THIS OR THAT?

With the curls of your hair
Cajoling your blue neck,
That which adorns your head
Shining brightly in the dark.
Your broad shoulders
Swaying this way and that,
You dance to the music
Of the night.

To the music
That comes from within you.
Sometimes—beats,
Sometimes in tunes.
A snake slithers by,
The one with horns stares in trance.

I know not who you are,

You could be This or That,

Hari or Hara. Should one really care?

ఇందు కల డందు లేడని
సందేహము వలదు చక్రి సర్వోపగతుం
డెందెందు వెదకి చూచిన
నందందే కలడు దానవాగ్రణి వింటే!
(పోతన భాగవతం, బమ్మెర పోతన)

indu kala ḍandu lēḍani
sandēhamu valadu cakri sarvōpagatum
ḍendendu vedaki cūcina
nandande kalaḍu dānavāgraṇi viñte!
(Pothana Bhāgavatam, Bammera Pothana)

In this, He is; in that, He is not—doubt not;
The one who holds the Chakra is inside everything,
Wherever you search and see,
There He is, O King of demons, listen!

∴

BHAKTA PRAHLADA

Have you ever seen the Lord run,
Hither and thither?
Have you ever seen Him run?

Traversing through clouds,
Seething into sand particles,
Moving across mountain ranges,
Unsure of where the child would
Point his tender finger,
He runs hither and thither.

Doorstep hovering with devotees,
Cries of conviction fresh in His ears,
The ever-reclining Lord—now runs,
Unsure of where the child would
Point his tender finger,
He runs hither and thither.

It ain't a great feat to catch him fall,
It ain't a great feat to save him from poison,
Now is the time to prove; so He runs,
Unsure of where the child would
Point his tender finger,
He runs hither and thither.

Insides—a blob of heated butter,
Raging like a lion on the outside,
Shuddering His mane—He runs,
Unsure of where the child would
Point his tender finger,
He runs hither and thither.

Oh, look at Him, the perpetual protector!
Oh, look at Him, the Victor of victors!
The ever-reclining Lord,
Whose feet are ever pampered,
Now runs
Hither and thither.

∴

...சிவன் கோலங் கண்டுன் கனல்செய் சினமும் விலகும்—கையைக்
கொஞ்சித் தொடுவாய் ஆனந்தக்கூத்திடுவாய்
அன்னை அன்னை...!
(சுப்பிரமணிய பாரதி)

...sivaṇ kōlaṅ kaṉduṇ kaṇalsei siṇamum vilagum—kaiyaik
koñchith thoduvāi āṇandhakkūththiduvāi!
aṇṇai aṇṇai...!
(Subramanya Bharathi)

On seeing Shiva's form, your apocalyptic rage vanishes;
You cajolingly clasp His hand and dance the Dance of Creation!
O Mother, O Mother!

∴

BIG BANG

Her forehead slightly tinted
With ashes from His chest;
Her neck gently tickled by
The slithering snake;
With the imprint of Rudraksha beads
On Her bosom,
And the fragrance of Kondrai flower
Still tantalising Her,
She slowly looks Him in the eye.

That magical moment,
The Universe is born.

∴

বিশ্বরূপের খেলা ঘরে
কতই গেলেম খেলে
অপরূপকে দেখে গেলেম
দুটি নয়ন মেলে।

পরশ যারে যায়না করা
সকল দেহে দিলেন ধরা...
(গীতাঞ্জলি, রবীন্দ্রনাথ ঠাকুর)

bisvarūper khelā ghare
katai gelem khele,
aparūpke dekhe gelem
duti naẏan mele |

paraś jāre jāẏnā karā
sakal dehe dilen dharā...
(Gitāñjali, Rabindranath Tagore)

This playhouse with infinite forms
Where I have played a lot,
That formless one–
I have seen with both my eyes.

That which is beyond touch
Has been trapped in my body...

∴

PARADOX

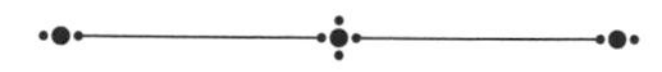

You are beyond language,
You are beyond communication.
Yet, You are the words we speak.
You transcend emotions,
You transcend feelings.
Yet, You are the love and the hate we feel.
You surpass forms,
You surpass shapes.
Yet, You are all that we see.
Unmarred by margins You are.
You are the uncontrollable stream.
You are this, You are that;
You are what lies between
This and that.
You are this, You are that;
You are that which could be
And that which quite couldn't.

காக்கை சிறகினிலே நந்தலாலா நின்றன்
கரியநிறம் தோன்றுதையே நந்தலாலா...
கேட்கும் ஒலியிலெல்லாம் நந்தலாலா
நின்றன் கீதம் இசைக்குதடா நந்தலாலா...
(சுப்பிரமணிய பாரதி)

kākkai si̱ragiṇilē nandhalālā niṇ̱raṇ
kariyani̱ram thōṇ̱rudhaiyē nandhalālā...
kētkum oliyilellām nandhalālā
niṇ̱raṇ gītham isaikkudhadā nandhalālā...
(Subramanya Bharathi)

In the wings of the crow, O dear one of Nanda,
your dark hue is seen...
In all the sounds, O dear one of Nanda,
your music is heard...

∴

WHEN HE ARRIVES

When the dark clouds emerged
And lightning struck my lovelorn eyes,
A vision I did see–
That of firm footsteps
Treading into the dense forest.

When the raindrops flocked
And embraced me one by one,
A vision I did see–
That of my gentle ears
Tickled by the coaxing breeze.

When dusk crept in slyly
And engulfed me from all sides,
A vision I did see–
That of an esoteric smile
On the luminous moon.

Taken aback
By the splendour of the sight,
I coyly closed my eyes.
And in that—a vision I did see.

That of the dark clouds—Your body,
Of the coaxing breeze—Your music,
Of the luminous moon—Your face,
Of the dense forest—my mind.

...சிவனவனென் சிந்தையுள் நின்ற அதனால்
அவனருளாலே அவன்தாள் வணங்கி...
(திருவாசகம்-சிவபுராணம், மாணிக்கவாசகர்)

...sivaṇavaṇeṇ sindhaiyul̲ niṇṟa adhaṇāl
avaṇarul̲ālē avaṇthāl̲ vaṉaṅgi...
(Thiruvāsagam-Sivapurāṉam, Manikkavasagar)

...As the Lord has rooted Himself in my thoughts,
I surrender at His feet, solely by His doing...

∴

SEA SHORE

In a dimly lit chamber
With hues not so sombre,
With haunting sounds of hymns
And some sudden whims.
The shore sees the sea;
Only the sea seizes the shore.

Bells boisterously ring,
Dozens of devotees sing.
Bodies begin to sway
This way, that way.
The shore sees the sea;
Only the sea seizes the shore.

Eyes begin to shudder,
Lips—a bit, quiver.
Insides of palms—wet,
On the forehead—beads of sweat.

The shore sees the sea;
Only the sea seizes the shore.

The queue begins to move
With heads turned back, askew.
To be with the sea forever and more,
They have to be, none but the shore.

The shore sees the sea;
Only the sea seizes the shore.

∴

बूँद समानी है समुंदर में, जानत है सब कोई ।
समुंदर समाना बूँद में, बूझे बिरला कोई ॥
(संत कबीर)

būnd samānī hai samundar mēṅ, jānat hai sab kōī ।
samundar samānā būnd mēṅ, būjhē birlā kōī ॥
(Sant Kabir)

When the drop becomes one with the ocean,
everyone understands it.
But, when the ocean becomes one with the drop,
a rare one alone understands it.

∴

THE CATCH

We played a game together,
She and i.
She opted to run first,
And made me seek Her.
i ran and ran,
As fast as i could.
i ran,
i gasped,
i tired out.
i couldn't catch Her. i lost.

Next, it was Her turn.
This time, She was to catch.
And i, to run, run and run.
i ran slowly; inch by inch.
i ran slowly so that
i would lose to Her.

She caught me: but, i didn't lose.

i won.

i was caught by Her.

i won.

∴

நானிலத்தில் பல பிறவி எடுத்து
திண்டாடியது போதாதா உந்தனுக்கு?
நான் ஒரு விளையாட்டு பொம்மையா
ஜகன்நாயகியே உமையே உந்தனுக்கு?
(பாபநாசம் சிவன்)

nāṇilaththil pala pi̱ravi eduththu
thin̠dādiyadhu pōdhādhā undhaṇukku?
nāṇ oru vi̱laiyāttu bommaiyā
jagaṇṇāyakiyē umaiyē undhaṇukku?
(Papanasam Sivan)

I have toiled taking several births in this world,
yet don't they suffice you?
Am I a playable toy to you,
O Goddess of the Universe, O Uma?

∴

DESTINATION

Only five more births I ask for,
Not one more than that, O Mother!
Only five more births I ask for,
None more, none more.

In the first birth, O Mother,
Make me your sparkling crown.
Your forehead shall touch mine,
In that, I shall quietly revel.

In the second birth, O Mother,
Could I be your shining necklace?
Resting my head on your caring bosom,
I shall revel, I shall revel.

In the third birth, O Mother,
Let me be your bangle.
Clasping your hand with grip,
Ah! In that I shall revel, I shall revel.

In the fourth birth, O Mother,
I shall be your graceful girdle.
Embracing you gently,
I shall revel, I shall revel.

In the fifth birth, O Mother,
Not much I ask for.
Just make me your anklet, O Mother.

So that, on your feet,
Forever, I shall revel.

NOTES ON POETS & TEXTS

Adi Shankaracharya

Shankara Bhagavatpada, the foremost Guru of Sanātana Dharma, expounded the Advaita (Non-dualism) philosophy along the length and breadth of India. Shankara was born in Kallady, a village in the southern Indian state of Kerala, to Aryamba and Shivaguru, and is believed to have lived in the first half of 8th century CE. He sought his mother's permission to take to Sanyāsa and went seeking his Guru, Govinda Bhagavatpada, along the river Narmada. The authorship of more than 300 texts, which include Bhāṣyas (commentaries), Prakaraṇa Granthas (original philosophical expositions) and Stōtras (devotional hymns), is attributed to Adi Shankaracharya. According to Shankara, Brahman alone is real and his works propound this Vēdānta backed by evidences from scriptures, reason, experiential knowledge and spiritual practices.

The lines on page 10 are taken from the second verse in Adi Shankara's *Dakṣiṇāmūrti Stōtram.*

Annamacharya

Tallapaka Annamayya or Annamacharya who lived in Tirupati in the 15th century is said to have composed a song a day for the 'God on the Hill'-Śrī Veṅkaṭēśvara (a manifestation of Mahā Viṣnu). A hallmark of Telugu Bhakti literature, Annamayya's avant-garde outpourings of love to the Lord spearheaded a new genre of poetry—the 'Padams'.

About thirteen thousand of his ocean of compositions are now stored on copper plates in a vault inside the temple. Characterised by lyrical musicality and a unique universality, his poems are majorly categorised as Śṛṅgāra (erotic) and Adhyātma (metaphysical).

Lines on page 38 and 52 are from his Adhyātma Kīrtanams taken from TTD's compilation of Annamacharya's Kīrtanams by Gadipeddi Ramasubbu Sharma.

Bammera Pothana

He is a Telugu poet of the 15th century, born in Bammera village, Andhra Pradesh. *Pothana Bhāgavatam*, a translation of *Bhāgavata Purāṇa* from Sanskrit to Telugu, is one of his best known works. An agriculturist by occupation, a scholar in Sanskrit and Telugu, Pothana's incidental conversion from Shaivism to Vaishnavism is said to have inspired him to translate Sage Vyasa's *Bhāgavatam*. Some of his other remarkable works include *Bhoginī Danḍakam* and *Vīrabhadra Vijayamu.*

The 275th poem from the *Saptama Skandam* of *Pothana Bhāgavatam* has been used on page 86 in this anthology.

Kabir

Sant Kabir was born in Benares, into a Muslim family that had recently converted into Islam. A revolutionary Bhakti poet of the fifteenth century, Kabir satirises the religious orthodoxies of Hinduism as well as Islam and expresses his love for One Deity.

This saint–poet is said to have been from the community of weavers and there are occasional references to his family profession in his poems too.

Lines on page 68 and 106 are extracts from Kabir's Dōhē. Some of Kabir's Dōhē are available in a bilingual edition *Essential Kabir*, translated by Arvind Krishna Mehrotra.

Lal Ded

Lal Ded or Lallesvari is a 14th century Kashmiri mystic whose works, which include about 258 Vākhs (verses), mark the beginning of modern Kashmiri literature. Born into a Brahmin family, she was married at the age of twelve and had a torturous domestic life with her husband and mother-in-law who were apathetic towards her spiritual inclinations. Lalla, as she addresses herself in her poems, would visit a nearby river each morning and would ferry across just to worship Naṭa Bhairava Kēśava. One day when she returned home from the river, with a pot of water on her head, her cruel husband who was poisoned by his mother's suspicions of Lalla's infidelity, struck the pot with a staff. The pot shattered, but the water is said to have remained frozen. She renounced her family at the age of 26 and became the disciple of a Shaiva Guru and later took to the life of a wandering mendicant. Her poems witness an evolution from that of uncertainty to a tone of epiphany gained through resilient reflection.

Sir George Grierson first published the English translations of Lalla's poems in 1920. Her Vākhs used on page 14 and 34 are Vākh 5 and Vākh 9 from Grierson's compilation. *I, LALLA-The Poems of Lal Ded* provides an extensive introduction to her life and Vākhs.

Mannikavasagar

He is a Tamil poet of the 9th century, whose *Thiruvāsagam* forms the 8th volume of *Thirumurai.* He was a minister to the Pandya King, Arimarthana Pandya of Madurai, and legend has it that he was given a huge sum of money by the king to buy horses for the king's cavalry.

On his way, Mannikavasagar is said to have met Lord Shiva who came in the guise of an ascetic. He attained enlightenment and soon built a temple for Shiva at Thiruperunthurai. *Thiruvembāvai* and *Thirupaḻḻiyezhuchi* on the Lord of Thiruperunthurai are also works of Mannikavasagar soaked in Bhakti and ardent love for the Lord.

The lines on page 102 are lines 19 and 20 from the first canto of *Thiruvāsagam.*

Papanasam Sivan

Papanasam Ramayya Sivan, a Vāggēyakāra—poet and composer—was born in 1890 in Thanjavur, South India. Sivan's given name was Ramayya and after the death of his mother Yogambal in 1910, he wandered from place to place, visiting temples and singing devotional songs. Ramayya soon became an active part of Neelakanda Sivan's music sessions and learnt many compositions from him. Since he visited Papanasam several times during this period, he came to be addressed as Papanasam Sivan.

His Bhakti-soaked compositions, characterised by lyrical simplicity and a rejuvenating musicality, are a regular in the Carnatic music and South Indian classical dance arenas till date. Papanasam Sivan has written and composed songs for many films in Tamil and Kannada too.

The lines on page 72 are from a song in the Tamil movie *Kuchēla* (1936) for which Sivan penned the lyrics and composed music. The excerpt on page 110 is from one of his famous compositions, 'Nāṇ oru viḻaiyāttu bommaiyā'.

Rabindranath Tagore

A Bengali writer, artist, social reformer and philosopher, born in 1861 in the then Calcutta, Tagore's literary works that include poems, short stories, essays and plays, have played a vital role in introducing the Indian culture to the West and vice versa. Tagore resisted orthodox linguistic structures and introduced new prose and poetry forms and incorporated colloquial Bengali language in his works. Spiritual yet simple, universal yet self expressive, Tagore's *Gītāñjali* (Song Offerings) is one of his most acclaimed works, which made him the first Non-European to win the Nobel Prize for Literature in 1913.

Lines on page 30 are taken from his poem 69 and the lines on page 94 are from poem 96 of the Rothenstein manuscript.

Samayōcita Padyamālikā

Samayōcita Padyamālikā is a compilation of wise maxims in Sanskrit by various authors. Subhāṣita is a genre of Sanskrit epigrammatic poems which are aphoristic in nature, covering a vast range of subjects.

The verse on page 22 is taken from *Samayōcita Padyamālikā* (page 53) published by Nirnaya Sagar Press, Mumbai.

Sirumanavoor Munusamy

Born in a village called Sirumanavoor or Sirumavoor in South India, Munusamy Mudaliyar is said to have spent several hours in the village temple in the presence of Natarāja and Ārūrammā, composing devotional hymns on them. One of his most well-known works, *Natarāja Paththu,* is a monologue of a devotee who questions the purpose of life with an irrefutable tone of intimacy with the Lord. Apart from being well versed in Tamil and Telugu poetry, he was also proficient in Siddha medicine, Śāstra, History, Astrology, Astronomy among other fields, and has penned several texts on these topics too.

Lines on page 48 are from stanza 3 of his *Natarāja Paththu.*

Subramanya Bharathi

Mahakavi Subramanya Bharathi—poet, writer, journalist, freedom fighter, was regarded as the 'morning star' of Tamil Renaissance and a pioneer of modern Tamil poetry. Born in 1882 in Thirunelveli district of the British India, Bharathi was a 'bard of freedom' who played a dual role of relieving Tamil language from the clutches of conservatism and freeing India from foreign dominance. Ranging from human emotions such as love and devotion, Bharathi's poems resonate with deep ideals such as pantheism and patriotism. In *Kaṉṉaṉ Pāttu*, he visualises the Lord as his friend, lover, mother, father, king, servant, child, playmate, Guru etc. Subramanya Bharathi has also penned poems in English which were compiled as 'Agni and Other Poems'.

Lines on page 60 are from a song in his *Thanippādalgaḻ* and the excerpt on page 90 is from *Ūzhikkūththu (Thōthira Pādalgaḻ)*. Lines on page 98 are from *Nandhalālā (Kaṉṉaṉ Pāttu)*.

Thirumoolar

Thirumoolar, originally known as Sundarar, was a Yogi residing in Mount Kailash. He is one of the 63 Nāyaṉmārs (Shaivite devotees) and is also one of the 8 Siddhars of Shaivism. It is said that Sundarar went on a journey to Podhigai Hills to meet Sage Agastya during which he saw a herd of cows stricken by sorrow around their dead cowherd, Moolan. Sundarar used his Yogic power and entered the body of the dead cowherd much to the delight of the cows. But when Sundarar returned to where he had left his own body, he was shocked to find that it had disappeared. The Yogi, by the divine will of Lord Shiva, continued to remain in the cowherd's body, immersed in deep penance under a peepal tree.

Soon, disciples flocked and he came to be addressed as Thirumoolar. His occasional outpourings came to be recorded, thus resulting in more than 3000 verses of the *Thirumandhiram* in which he lays a religious and spiritual path that delineates the devotional, philosophical, Yogic, Tantric, Siddhanthic tenets of Shaivism.

Verse 2290 which comes under the eighth *Thandhiram* of *Thirumandhiram* is found on page 26 in this anthology.

Thiruvalluvar

Thiruvalluvar is a saint–poet, believed to have lived during the 1st century BC or 6th century AD. His magnum opus *Thirukkuṟaḻ* stands the test of time owing to its universal and practical wisdom in the form of 1330 couplets or Kuraḻs, with exactly seven words in each couplet, that are divided into three books—*Aṟaththuppāl* (Book of Virtue), *Porutppāl* (Book of Wealth) and *Iṇbaththupāl* (Book of Love). Ranging from topics such as domestic virtue, ascetic virtue, destiny, politics, limbs of the state, clandestine love and wedded love, the couplets are perennial maxims that make *Thirukkuṟaḻ* a treatise of all times. The couplet on page 18 is Kuraḻ 331 which comes under *Aṟaththuppāl*—the book of virtue.

Valmiki muni

Sage Valmiki is known as the Ādi Kavi or the first poet as he authored the Ādi Kavyā (first Sanskrit poem) *Rāmāyaṇa* in 24,000 verses. Valmiki's *Rāmāyaṇa* is usually dated between 500 BC to 100 BC, but it is also said that Sita took refuge in Valmiki Ashram where Lava and Kusha were born, making the sage a contemporary of Lord Rama, thus adding further ambiguity to his period. Legend has it that Sage Valmiki was born as Ratnakara and raised by a hunter. As he got married and his family grew larger, Ratnakara found it difficult to feed them and hence resorted to robbery. His life transformed completely when he met Sage Narada in the forest and was taught the sacred name of 'Rama' by him. Ratnakara, as per the instructions of Sage Narada, sat in meditation chanting the Lord's name until he was covered by an ant hill.

Narada rewarded his penance and named him 'Valmiki'—the one reborn from the Valmīka (ant hill). It is said that the great sage composed the *Rāmāyaṇa* after he received a divine vision from Lord Brahma asking him to write the epic in verse form.

The extract on page 56 is verse 33 in the 15th Sarga or chapter of *Sundara Kāṇḍaṃ* (Book 5) of Valmiki's *Rāmāyaṇa*.

Vyasa muni

Krishna Dvaipayana is known to have compiled and classified the Vēdas in the end of the Dvāpara Yuga, thus obtaining the name Vyasa or Vēda Vyasa. He is the author of the *Mahābhārata,* according to which he was the son of Satyavati, a fisherwoman and sage Parashara.

It is said that he was born on an island and so named Krishna Dvaipayana, referring to his dark complexion and birth place. The *Bhagavad Gītā* is a part of *Mahābhārata,* which consists of 18 chapters with a total of about 700 verses, set in the context of the Dharma Yuddha between the Pandavas and Kauravas.

The verse on page 44 is from chapter 18 (*Mōkṣa Sanyāsa Yōga*—verse 46) and the verse on page 64 is from chapter 10 (*Vibhūti Yōga*—verse 20).

Yajurvēda

The *Yajurvēda* contains a set of Mantras (sacred hymns) to be recited during rituals. The word 'Yajus' means worship and this Vēda serves as a guide to worship rituals. The *Yajurvēda* is broadly classified into *'Kṛṣṇa Yajurvēda'* and *'Śukla Yajurvēda'* and Vyasa is said to be the compiler of the Vēdas.

The verse on page 82 is from the *Sandhyā Vandana* (a ritual paying salutation to twilight) Mantras in the *Yajurvēda.*

ACKNOWLEDGEMENTS

Some have consciously helped in the birth of this book, and some others, unconsciously have.

Incorporating excerpts from the literatures of regional languages of India was possible only because of the generous help extended by experts in the languages. My respectful thanks to Dr. S. Raghuraman (Tamil scholar) and Dr. Advaitavadini Kaul, (scholar in Kashmiri philosophy, culture & historiography), for magnanimously sharing their knowledge and clarifying my doubts with regards to the Tamil and Kashmiri verses respectively. Heartfelt thanks to Sri Jaikishore Mosalikanti and Dr. Anupama Kylash for helping me with the Telugu verses, and Dr. Srabani Bhattacharyya (Assistant Professor, Dept. of Hindi, Stella Maris College), for guiding me through the Hindi and Bengali verses.

My sincere thanks to Sri Uttiya Barua for patiently explaining the poems of Tagore and diligently proofreading the Bengali script. Thanks to Sri Ashok Lahiri and Smt. Amrita Lahiri for enhancing my understanding of the Bengali verses and to Smt. Emani Soujanya for monitoring the Sanskrit verses.

I have been fortunate to have had Smt. Sharanya Bharathwaj and my dear friend, Meghna N Lokabhirama Raju proofread the manuscript meticulously with utmost attention to every minute detail. I truly value the contributions of Dr. Sheela Unnikrishnan, Dr. Kuldeep M Pai and Smt. Padmavani Mosalikanti, in proofreading the Tamil, Sanskrit and

Hindi verses respectively.

My sincere thanks—to Sammohana Mosalikanti, for capturing pictures of Meghna Unnikrishnan's sketches with care and sensitivity; to Hamsika Ravichandran, for stepping in at the right time and effortlessly lubricating the final stages of the designing process; to Notion Press, for understanding my ideas and ideals; to Rajadarshini Saravanan, for helping me with arriving at a layout for the book in the initial stages; to Meghna's parents—Smt. Manju M. Nair & Sri P. R. Unnikrishnan, for supporting her in this endeavour.

The threads that bind a book are many, yet each thread is significant in holding the book together. I am grateful to all those who trust in my writing, especially to Sheela ma'am and Kuldeep Anna, for giving me ample opportunities to awaken the writer in me.

Made in the USA
Monee, IL
03 November 2021

81348068R00081